MIDLOTHIAN PUBLIC LIBRARY

3 1614 00195 9510

W9-BIJ-588

THE LAYERS OF EARTH'S ATMOSPHERE

ELIZABETH BORNGRABER

PowerKiDS press

MIDLOTHIAN PUBLIC LIBRARY
14701 S. KENTON AVENUE
MIDLOTHIAN, IL 60445

New York

JUN
551.51
BOR

Published in 2019 by The Rosen Publishing Group, Inc.
29 East 21st Street, New York, NY 10010

Copyright © 2019 by The Rosen Publishing Group, Inc.

All rights reserved. No part of this book may be reproduced in any form without permission in writing from the publisher, except by a reviewer.

Editor: Rachel Gintner
Cover Design: Michael Flynn
Interior Layout: Rachel Rising

Photo Credits: Cover Aphelleon/Shutterstock.com; Cover, pp. 3, 4, 6, 8, 9, 10, 11, 12, 13, 14, 15, 16, 17, 18, 20, 21, 22, 23, 24 (background) chaowat kawera/Shutterstock.com; p. 5 shooarts/Shutterstock.com; p. 7 (insert) https://commons.wikimedia.org/wiki/File:Murchison_meteorite_0.459g.jpg; p. 7 (background) Stocktrek Images/Stocktrek Images/Getty Images; pp. 8, 10, 14, 16, 20 gritsalak karalak/Shutterstock.com; p. 9 Wildnerdpix/Shutterstock.com; p. 11 Culture Club/Contributor/Getty Images; p. 12 Yuri_Arcurs/DigitalVision/Getty Images; p. 13 Courtesy of NASA Image and Video Library; p. 15 Juhku/Shutterstock.com; p. 17 AuntSpray/Shutterstock.com; p.19 Arctic-Images/Stone/Getty Images; p. 21 Science & Society Picture Library/Contributor/Getty Images; p. 22 Rawpixel.com/Shutterstock.com.

Library of Congress Cataloging-in-Publication Data

Names: Borngraber, Elizabeth, author.
Title: The layers of Earth's atmosphere / Elizabeth Borngraber.
Description: New York : PowerKids Press, [2019] | Series: Spotlight on weather and natural disasters | Includes bibliographical references and index.
Identifiers: LCCN 2018006091| ISBN 9781508169154 (library bound) | ISBN 9781508169178 (pbk.) | ISBN 9781508169185 (6 pack)
Subjects: LCSH: Atmosphere--Juvenile literature. | Weather--Juvenile literature. | Meteorology--Juvenile literature. | Earth (Planet)--Juvenile literature.
Classification: LCC QC863.5 .B665 2018 | DDC 551.51--dc23
LC record available at https://lccn.loc.gov/2018006091

Manufactured in the United States of America

CPSIA Compliance Information: Batch #CS18PK For further information contact Rosen Publishing, New York, New York at 1-800-237-9932.

CONTENTS

CHAPTER ONE

WHAT'S THE ATMOSPHERE?

The atmosphere is a blanket of gases that covers our planet. It's mostly nitrogen and oxygen—oxygen being the gas we need to breathe. There's also water vapor in the atmosphere. Water vapor is water in gas form.

The atmosphere is very important. It protects us from things such as the harmful effects of the sun's rays or rocks that fall from outer space. It can stop or slow down these rocks that travel toward Earth.

Like Earth, the atmosphere has layers. These are the troposphere, stratosphere, mesosphere, thermosphere, and exosphere. Each layer is separate but has its own special features. All of the layers play a part in keeping Earth a safe and comfortable place to live. Without them, life on our planet would not be able to survive.

LAYERS OF THE ATMOSPHERE

EXOSPHERE
430 to 6,200 miles (692 to 9,978 km)

aurora

satellite

THERMOSPHERE
53 to 430 miles (85 to 692 km)

Hubble
telescope

MESOSPHERE
32 to 53 miles (52 to 85 km)

meteors

STRATOSPHERE
6 to 32 miles (10 to 52 km)

fighter jet

airplane

balloon

TROPOSPHERE
About 6 miles (10 km)

Each layer of the atmosphere is special. This picture shows
the distance of each layer from Earth.

CHAPTER TWO

EARLY ATMOSPHERE

Earth's atmosphere has changed over billions of years. When Earth first formed, there was very little atmosphere. It was very hot and there was no oxygen in the air to breathe. As Earth cooled, volcanoes spit gases such as carbon dioxide into the air.

Oxygen is thought to have formed from interactions in our oceans. As time passed, carbon dioxide **dissolved** into the water, where tiny bacteria lived. These bacteria used water, sunlight, and carbon dioxide to make energy. This process is known as photosynthesis. As they did this, they likely freed oxygen into the atmosphere. Oxygen in the atmosphere increased. Carbon dioxide decreased. Other gases made by the volcanoes broke apart. Lighter gases escaped into outer space. This left Earth with the beginnings of the atmosphere we know today.

**MURCHISON
METEORITE**

The basic stuff of life may have come from outer space. The 1969 Murchison meteorite, for instance, had **particles** of organic matter on its surface. A meteorite is a piece of rock or metal that falls from outer space through the atmosphere and lands on Earth.

CHAPTER THREE

TROPOSPHERE

The troposphere is the layer of the atmosphere that's closest to Earth's surface. It extends about 6 miles (10 km) from the ground toward outer space. It's shorter in length at the North and South Poles and longer at the equator. Almost all Earth's weather happens in the troposphere. This is because it holds most of the water vapor in the atmosphere. This vapor is needed for the formation of clouds and rain.

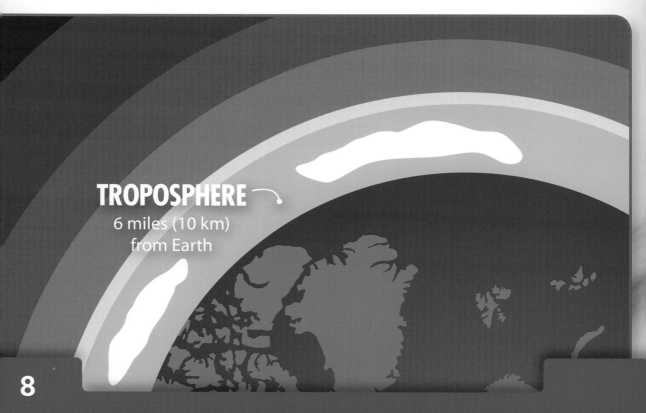

TROPOSPHERE
6 miles (10 km)
from Earth

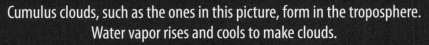
Cumulus clouds, such as the ones in this picture, form in the troposphere. Water vapor rises and cools to make clouds.

Temperatures in the troposphere change with **altitude**. The higher the air, the colder it gets. This is because the air also gets thinner. Air thins when gas **molecules** spread out. Because higher altitudes have thinner air, there's also less oxygen. People who climb tall mountains sometimes carry extra oxygen with them because there isn't enough to breathe at the top of the mountain.

CHAPTER FOUR

STRATOSPHERE

The layer after the troposphere is the stratosphere. Like the troposphere, the depth of this layer varies. It can range from 5 miles to 24 miles (8.1 to 38.6 km) thick. That's the length of over 350 football fields! The air in this layer is less **dense** than in the troposphere. This layer also has less water vapor. Because there's less water in the air, few clouds form and it's generally calm. Most airplanes fly here. Thinner air means they can fly quite fast.

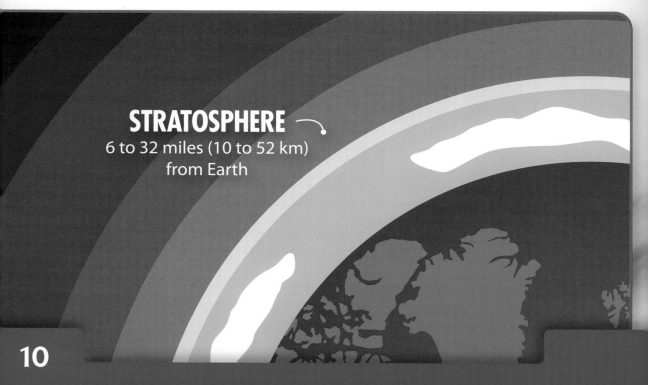

STRATOSPHERE
6 to 32 miles (10 to 52 km)
from Earth

In 1931, Auguste Piccard, right, and Paul Kipfer were the first humans to fly in the stratosphere. They flew in a balloon Piccard created.

Very few birds can fly at this height. The Rüppell's griffon vulture is the highest-flying bird in the world. This vulture can fly as high as 36,000 feet (10,972.8 m) in the air. That's as high as most airplanes fly. This bird can fly at this height because it doesn't need as much oxygen as other animals.

CHAPTER FIVE

THE OZONE LAYER

An important part of the stratosphere is the **ozone** layer. This layer of ozone gas helps protect Earth from the sun. When the sun's light enters the atmosphere, it includes ultraviolet rays, or UV rays. Too much exposure to UV rays can hurt your skin and make you sick. This is why you put hats, sunglasses, and sunscreen on when you go outside. The ozone layer is like a huge blanket of sunscreen. It protects us by **absorbing** UV rays, stopping them from reaching Earth's surface.

1979   2016

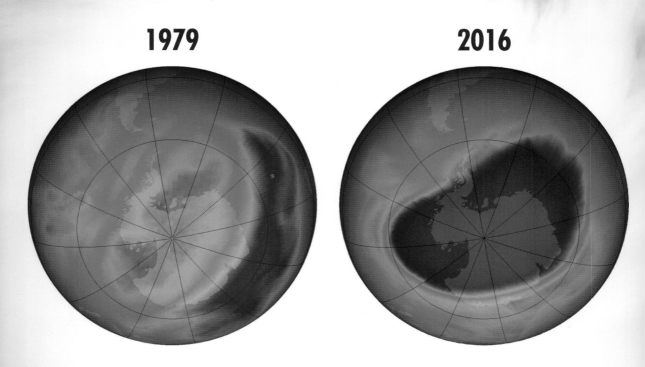

It's very important to protect the ozone layer. Without it, plants, animals, and people wouldn't be able to live on Earth. However, people harmed the ozone layer with chemicals called CFCs. After we learned how bad CFCs were, most people stopped using them.

CHAPTER SIX

MESOSPHERE

The mesosphere is above the stratosphere. We know the least about this layer. It's too high for airplanes and too low for **satellites** or spacecraft. This makes it hard to gather information about this layer. However, we do know that the mesosphere is the coldest layer. It can reach -184°F (-120°C). This is colder than the coldest temperature ever recorded on Earth, which was -135.8°F (-93.2°C) in Antarctica in 2010. The mesosphere is also home to the highest clouds in the atmosphere. Clouds in this layer are made of frozen water vapor.

MESOSPHERE
32 to 53 miles (52 to 85 km) from Earth

These ice clouds formed in the mesosphere.
They can only be seen after sunset.

This layer also plays an important part in keeping Earth safe. Every day, particles of rock fly toward Earth. As they go through the atmosphere, they hit molecules in the mesosphere and burn up. If an object is larger, it may pass through this layer and hit Earth.

CHAPTER SEVEN

THERMOSPHERE

The thermosphere is the thickest layer in the atmosphere. It also has the highest temperatures. This is because gases in the thermosphere absorb UV rays and other rays from the sun. This speeds up gas molecules and increases their temperature. This layer can get up to 2,732°F (1,500°C). You would need a very special thermometer to measure temperatures this high! Even though the temperature is high, you wouldn't feel hot. Actually, it would feel very cold since heat is created when energy passes between molecules, and molecules in this layer are too far apart to pass heat to you.

THERMOSPHERE
53 to 430 miles (85 to 692 km) from Earth

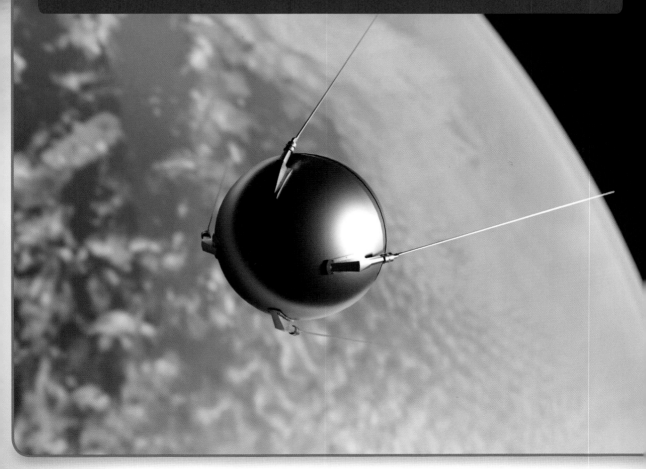

Sputnik I was the first satellite to reach orbit in the layer just after the thermosphere—the ionosphere. It reached a distance of 584 miles (939.9 km) from Earth's surface. Russia launched it on October 4, 1957.

The gas molecules are so far apart that this layer is more like outer space. In fact, some satellites **orbit** the Earth in the thermosphere. Scientists use these satellites to study things about our planet and outer space.

CHAPTER EIGHT

DANCING LIGHTS

The ionosphere is a gas layer full of ions that includes the thermosphere and parts of the mesosphere and exosphere. X-rays and UV rays from the sun create ions, which are particles that have charges. On the far side of the ionosphere is the magnetosphere. This layer protects the atmosphere from solar wind, which is the flow of charged particles from the sun.

In places where the ionosphere and magnetosphere overlap, an interesting and beautiful event can occur. Particles from solar wind end up in the ionosphere and run into ions. When they hit, they create colorful **auroras** in the night sky. Some people call these dancing lights. Auroras happen around the North and South Poles, so they're also called the northern and southern lights. Auroras can be red, orange, yellow, green, and blue.

Green is the most common aurora color. This color happens when ions hit oxygen low in the atmosphere.

CHAPTER NINE

EXOSPHERE

Our atmosphere ends with the exosphere. This layer is where the atmosphere becomes outer space. Scientists don't agree exactly where the exosphere ends and where outer space begins. Molecules in this layer are very far apart. This makes the air very thin. Gravity will pull most of these molecules into lower atmospheric levels, but some molecules escape into space. In the exosphere, Earth's pull on them isn't very strong. Because the air is so thin, many weather satellites orbit here. These satellites can get a clear view of Earth from this height.

EXOSPHERE

430 to 6,200 miles
(692 to 9,978 km)
from Earth

Astronaut John W. Young took this photo during the Apollo 16 lunar mission. Only special cameras can record the geocorona.

The geocorona is the upper edge of the exosphere. In pictures, it looks like a blue ring of light that circles Earth. When the sun's UV rays bounce off gases in the exosphere, they cause this light.

CHAPTER TEN

JUST RIGHT

The atmosphere can tell us a lot about the history of our planet. It also makes Earth the only place we know of where people can live. The Goldilocks **theory** is the idea that only planets with just the right conditions can support life. Earth is at the perfect distance from the sun to support life. Venus is too close. Mars is too far. But Earth is just right.

Every layer of Earth's atmosphere works together to keep Earth safe and comfortable. Because of this, it's very important that we work to protect the atmosphere. You can do this by walking or biking to decrease the exhaust that cars create. You can also reuse or recycle things to decrease waste. You can plant more trees. All of these things can help protect the atmosphere.

GLOSSARY

absorb (uhb-ZORB) To take in.

altitude (AL-tuh-tood) The height of something above a certain level.

aurora (uh-ROH-ruh) The lights that shine in Earth's atmosphere under some conditions.

dense (DEHNS) Tightly packed.

dissolve (dih-ZAHLV) To break down and spread out in a liquid.

molecule (MAH-luh-kyool) The smallest possible amount of something that has all the characteristics of that thing.

orbit (OHR-buht) To travel around something in a curved path. Also the curved path something follows around a planet, sun, or another thing.

ozone (OH-zohn) A form of oxygen found in a layer high in Earth's atmosphere.

particle (PAR-tih-kuhl) A small piece of something.

satellite (SAA-tuh-lyte) A spacecraft placed in orbit around Earth, a moon, or a planet to collect information or for communication.

theory (THEER-ee) An idea suggested or presented as possibly true but that is not known or proven to be true.

INDEX

PRIMARY SOURCE LIST

Page 7
Specimen of the Murchison meteorite. Carbonaceous chondrite made of silicates, metal, and sulfide. September 28, 1969.

Page 11
Paul Kipfer and Auguste Piccard. Photograph. September 1930. Musée du Léman.

Page 21
Enhanced ultraviolet view of the geocorona. Photograph. John W. Young. April 21,1972. NASA.

WEBSITES

Due to the changing nature of Internet links, PowerKids Press has developed an online list of websites related to the subject of this book. This site is updated regularly. Please use this link to access the list: www.powerkidslinks.com/swnd/atmos